Transition Living

insights from 1 Samuel for the 3rd millennium church

Stephen Gaukroger

@Goldhill

THE WORD MADE FRESH!

discussion starters for small groups

Transition Living:*insights from 1 Samuel for the 3rd millennium church*

A **scriptureunion@goldhill** product published by Scripture Union, 207–209 Queensway, Bletchley, MK2 2EB, UK. This imprint is especially created to bring the ministry of Gold Hill Baptist Church to a wider audience.

Scripture Union is an international Christian charity working with churches in more than 130 countries providing resources to bring the good news about Jesus Christ to children, young people and families – and to encourage them to develop spiritually through the Bible and prayer. As well as a network of volunteers, staff and associates who run holidays, church-based events and school Christian groups, SU produces a wide range of publications and supports those who use their resources through training programmes.

Email: info@scriptureunion.org.uk Internet: www.scriptureunion.org.uk

Scripture Union Australia
Locked Bag 2, Central Coast Business Centre, NSW 2252 222 Internet: www.su.org.au

Gold Hill: Gold Hill is a Baptist Church and member of the Evangelical Alliance. Their mission statement is: Equipping God's people, Serving God's Son, Reaching God's World. The church meets at Gold Hill Common East, Chalfont St Peter, SL9 9DG. Stephen Gaukroger is the senior pastor.

Email: office@goldhill.org.uk Internet: www.goldhill.org.uk

© Stephen Gaukroger 2004
First published 2004

ISBN 1 84427 040 8

Quotations from the New International Version of the Holy Bible, © 1973, 1978, 1984 by International Bible Society, used by permission of Hodder and Stoughton Limited.

British Library Cataloguing-in-Publication Data: a catalogue record for this book is available from the British Library.

Cover design by aricot vert of Fleet.

Internal design by David Lund Design.

Printed and bound by Ebenezer Baylis, The Trinity Press, Worcester.

Scripture Union: Using the Bible to inspire children, young people and adults to know God

Transition Living
insights from 1 Samuel
for the 3rd millennium church
Intro

Many parts of our world are in a state of transition as this third millennium opens. From the large arena of international politics and big business right through to the unmarked and uncertain daily lives of thousands of individuals in our planet's many and varied nations, the current agenda is typically one of massive change and the climate frequently a loss of confidence and equilibrium.

Samuel, Saul and David were giants of the Old Testament who, like us, lived in days of transition and crisis. They lived in the era of change between the days of authority from a succession of judges and the appointment of a line of kings. From being 12 tribes searching for identity, the people of Israel were undergoing the painful metamorphosis of becoming a fully-fledged nation.

The same issues of identity that they struggled with are confronting many countries today, not least as they affect key issues of national currency, sovereignty, immigration, trade, defence and so on.

Culturally, many parts of the western world are in enormous decay. Political structures are falling apart – and people have lost so much trust in them that democratic rights to vote and affect decisions are regarded with apathy. Morally we are in decline. Clear ethical guidelines are a thing of the past. In 20 years from now, will marriage still exist? If so, in what form? What will family life look like?

What will our city streets look like, with the continuing erosion of respect for authority? What kinds of governments will manage societies that reel from crisis to crisis?

The Bible says that in the days of 1 Samuel every man did what was right in his own eyes. What a perfect description of our own third millennium days!

You may argue that we've been here before. Perhaps in your lifetime or your parents'. Yes, the period immediately following the Second World War was, to some extent, a time of transition. But, though there was poverty and pain, enormous distress of bereavement and loss, there was still a degree of certainty. There was a 'settledness' about the superpowers and the nation states.

Today there is no underlying sense of 'settledness'. The accelerated pace of today's life adds to our uncertainty. We commute through life as if on some out-of-control conveyor belt, running headlong though all the major transition points of education, career, relationships, children, retirement.

Yet, into both our cultural and personal transition the God of 1 Samuel speaks words of certainty, direction and affirmation. Let's learn together!

Stephen Gaukroger

How to get the best out of **the Word made fresh!**

This series of **the Word made fresh!** discussion starters for small groups provides thought-provoking teaching from Stephen Gaukroger with questions to stimulate discussion and prayer.

The material will suit groups wanting to think about biblical principles as they affect and challenge contemporary life – particularly groups wanting to explore all this within a fairly unstructured programme. It is suitable for newly-formed or established or mixed groups, of about six to 14 members, with limited or extensive Bible knowledge.

It will be helpful if the group leader has had some experience of leading and some understanding of group dynamics, as working with the free format of **the Word made fresh!** will be stretching. Particular attention will need to be paid to involving everyone in the discussion, and avoiding the domination of the conversation by one or two people. It will be a real asset if the group leader has spent time getting to know the members as individuals so that he or she can more readily identify topics which need particularly sensitive handling. That said, the format requires little preparation for the leader apart from a thorough reading of the teaching section and some advance thinking about the questions and Bible verses.

All group members need their own copy of this workbook. Where group members can commit to reading both the Bible passages and the study material in advance of meeting together this can be a real advantage – the group leader need only recall the main points. But if this is not practical, another approach to getting the best out of the material would be to spend 10 to 15 minutes having the study material read aloud by one or more people at the beginning of the session, perhaps in the relaxed setting of coffee and doughnuts.

The worksheet will guide discussion and is intended to be completed during the session. However, the purpose of the time together will be largely fulfilled if the group members have interacted

- with the teaching;
- with the Bible verses;
- with each other in expressing their thoughts and
- with God in prayer.

So completing the worksheet fully or neatly with the 'right' answers is not a criterion for judging the group time! Some people will find it helpful as a record of their thoughts and the discussion, while others will find it a hindrance. Feel free!

Transition Living
1: Clash of dynasties
1 Samuel 1–3

The action at the opening of 1 Samuel takes place some 30 miles north west of Jerusalem, although Jerusalem at that time was not much of a city.

We hear of a man called Elkanah – a devout, religious man – with two wives. One wife, Hannah, had no children. But the other, Peninnah, produced them as easily as shelling peas! Bigamy was not uncommon in those days, particularly for wealthy men, because of the emphasis on producing a son – a fundamental concern for Jews. Failure to produce children was sad, implying the judgement of God. But, importantly, it meant the failure to produce a son and heir.

Despite her childlessness, Elkanah feels tenderness and affection for Hannah (1:5). But the situation leads to terrible family stress (1:6). This is not a happy family. Peninnah is behaving in what could be described as a 'bitchy' way with her fellow-wife – irritating and provoking her: 'Look! I'm giving birth to all these children,

the situation led to terrible family stress

what's wrong with *you*?' It is enormously difficult for Hannah – and probably difficult for Elkanah, having his wives warring in this way. It is not simply a brief squabble needing to be patched up but a long-running irritation (1:7).

Elkanah doesn't always respond well. With perhaps typical male frustration he would say (1:8), 'Don't I mean more to you than ten sons?' Husbands are not always sensitive to their wives' needs. 'Look dear, you've got *me*, what more do you want?' But 'In bitterness of soul Hannah wept much and prayed to the Lord' (1:10). This is a family in transition about to play a key part in a nation in transition – and the woman in trouble at the centre of the storm gives us a wonderful key to what to do when in crisis. *She prays.*

In her praying she offers the son she is longing for to God as someone set apart for him. She is passionate, she agonises, her lips moving as she prays in the desperation of that incredible urge to have a child.

If you follow the story through you will see that her passionate prayer is answered by a partnership of the human and the divine. Because we are influenced by so much of the secular world view, our first port of call in trouble is nearly always a *human* solution. When we are sick we think immediately of a pill. Have we financial concerns? We seek a financial adviser. Legal matters? We find a lawyer. All

Have we understood that all of life is a divine and human partnership?

perfectly legitimate – but the danger is in the mindset that this is where life's solutions lie, and that the only times we need to seek God are for overtly *spiritual* concerns.

But here the solution is both divine and human. Hannah prays, and she and her husband sleep together (1:19). That's a principle of cooperation with God that we need to adopt.

So, will we come God in passionate prayer about the state of our culture in crisis and transition? When we are worried about our own transitions – starting college or a new job, facing family breakdown, coping with life alone after bereavement – do we seek God with Hannah's passion? Have we understood that *all* of life is a divine and human partnership? We need the divine stamp of miracle in our lives, but we must partner with that miracle. And we also need the partnership of others who belong to Christ. Frequently I talk with people whose lives have shipwrecked. They have drifted away from God and from God's people. The truth is, we need each other.

So Samuel arrives, and when he is weaned – which in that culture is more likely to mean that he is a boy of about

four or five years old rather than a baby or toddler – he is taken to the Temple (1:24). Hannah fulfils her promise to God. How often do we promise but not deliver? In a crisis we promise God a great deal. Even atheists cry out to God when their plane is going down! The promise lasts only until the safe landing on the airport tarmac.

Hannah's gratitude is summed up in 1:27. And 1:28 shows the extent of her promise, that Samuel will be given to the Lord 'for his whole life'. Every day, without exception, is to be God's.

If you get to 70 or 80 or 90 years of age, and are still following God, you're someone to be honoured as a 'whole life' disciple. But 'whole life' does not just mean every day. It means the whole of what it means to be alive. Samuel's social life, his spiritual life, his leisure, his thought life – every bit was to be God's. Sometimes we are just hanging onto God by our fingertips and most of our experiences go on without him. We worship God on Sunday and forget him Monday to Saturday, trying to be spiritually anonymous in our workplaces, homes, colleges. Many people think God is not interested in their office experience or their factory experience or their relationships. This is completely untrue. God is interested in our whole lives *for* the whole of our lives.

When a man or woman determines to dedicate *their whole life* and *the whole of their life* to the service of the King, they are going to be able to straddle the transitions this world is going through; they are going to be able to cope with massive cultural shifts; they are going to be strong through any turmoil in their personal lives.

Samuel was born at a time of transition – the end of the period of the judges and the beginning of the period of the kings in Jewish history. And that contrast of cultures

We long to see our culture changed –

is represented by the two families or dynasties – the children of Hannah and the children of Eli.

God is here judging the old dynasty – Eli's children – and saying that it has failed; it is corrupt. And he is endorsing the new dynasty. His judgement is on the sick and perverted ways of the past, and his justice comes in the shape of Samuel.

If only we could be part of God's judgement and justice on our own times, in our own country! We want to cry out against the corrupt nature of our culture; to cry to God to raise up Samuels throughout the land who will epitomise a new cultural model of holiness and bring about a paradigm shift. We long to see our culture reformed, changed – renewed in its politics, its economics, its social structures.

We read that 'In those days the word of the Lord was rare; there were not many visions' (3:1). The old dispensation, that of Eli and his kind, was pretty poverty-stricken in terms of divine intervention. Like our world today. It's discouraging to monitor international news stories and reflect on the absence of God, of his Word, of his standards. We see bloodshed, rioting, brutalising torture of the innocent, lying and corruption in the arenas of power. It seems incredible that God continues to withhold his hand of judgement! As Ruth Graham said on one occasion, 'If God doesn't judge us in the West soon, he'll have to apologise to Sodom and Gomorrah!' Martin Luther, looking at his world in the 1500s, said, 'If I were as our Lord God and these vile people were as disobedient as now they be, I would smash the world in pieces.' He, too, wondered how God could withhold his hand.

Why is God restraining his hand from our culture which is so obviously decadent? It may be because he wants the Word of the Lord to go from being 'rare' (3:1) to being as prevalent and powerful as it was by the end of that chapter. Is he restraining his hand for an opportunity for revival to sweep through the land before judgement?

Samuel first hears the voice of God in the Temple as a child (3:4). There is a growing desperation in Samuel as he hears the voice of God not once, nor twice, but three times. 'You called me… You called me!… You *did* call me!' Then Eli realises what is happening and encourages him to respond to God and listen (3:9). God has some pretty disturbing news for Eli and his family – not that it was entirely new for Eli, since God had already warned about the coming judgement (2:31–34). Samuel, for whom it is news, is reluctant to give the message.

Perhaps you feel that God's judgement on Eli's family is harsh. But we go on to learn that Eli has been involved in his sons' sinfulness. In the ancient world there was a much closer link between father and children in terms of obedience. There was strong expectation that sons would adopt wholesale the standards of the parent, and live them out – so different from our culture where there is a strong expectation that children will rebel against their parents' standards.

There are strong parallels between Eli's dynasty and today's world which are indicators of coming judgement. We read (2:12–16) that Eli's sons have no regard for God, and that they act like gangsters – guilty of greed, materialism, corruption and extortion. They use their position as priests for their own ends, powerfully manipulating those around them, including seducing powerless women. Instead of modelling good leadership they model selfish greed. Like the majority of people of the third millennium, they are always seeking to acquire. We, too, are constantly dissatisfied with what we've got. We continually compare ourselves with others and have an overwhelming need to

reformed, renewed in its politics,
its economics, its social structures

own the latest and the best. We define ourselves by our purchases. And we are sexually promiscuous. What a tragedy that so many of us, even Christians, have bought into Eli's dynasty!

to speak out because it sounds so judgemental, so negative, so damning. But we read (3.20) that everyone recognises that Samuel is a true prophet. He is anointed, that is touched by the power of the Spirit to do his work, and 'attested', meaning confirmed in that work by God.

We need to learn what it is to be doormats for God. Too many of us are going about our lives and careers seeking the best for ourselves, with God as a kind of optional add-on

Eli's sons (2:25) don't listen to their father or to God. They are on a hedonistic binge. It's Samuel who listens carefully. A sure sign of moral decay is when people listen to no other voices but their own.

But Eli is also implicated. He not only condones their sins but participates in it (2:29). He's guilty by association, not some kind of innocent bystander. And so are we, the nations of the West, guilty – implicated in the terminal decay of our culture.

Like Noah before him, Samuel is to be part of God's judgement. This begins with Samuel's submission to God's purposes, which is in direct contrast to the arrogant self-assertion of Eli's sons. We need to learn what it is to be doormats for God. Too many of us are going about our lives and careers seeking the best for ourselves, with God as a kind of optional add-on. We acknowledge his presence. We're glad he's around. We hope he blesses our plans, but if he doesn't we'll plough on trying to achieve something, with God hanging on to our coat tails. Submission is a characteristic of spiritual maturity, a characteristic of the new dynasty that God wants to raise up, where people are submissive to *God*, not actively rebellious against him.

Samuel is prepared to submit to God, even if it means telling Eli an unpalatable message. The truth can be hard

Let's pray that, as Eli's dynasty dies, God will raise up a whole new generation on this cusp of the third millennium which will see the church go forward with power, and the Word of God penetrate the whole earth.

Transition Living Worksheet

1: Clash of dynasties
1 Samuel 1–3

1 What symptoms can you identify which would suggest that we live in a culture in transition? Make a list on your own and then compare it with those of others in the group.

_____

_____

_____

2 What do you think is the pain of the childless couple in today's society, compared to Hannah's grief?

_____

• What do you think of the hope offered by contemporary medical procedures?

_____

• How can the church help?

_____

_____

3 What do you think about the balance in 1 Samuel 1 between trusting God and being yourself part of the answer to a need?

_____

• Can you think of any illustrations of this in your own experience or the experience of someone you know?

_____

_____

4 What lessons are there in 1 Samuel 1 about gratitude?

_____

• And about handling disappointment?

_____

_____

_____

5 To what extent are we – like Eli – limited by our own expectations of the way God does or does not act?

_____

_____

_____

6 Do you give God opportunity to speak into your life? Pray as a group about the barriers to hearing God that you face
• as individuals;
• as a group;
• in the local church.

7. Parental responsibility – when will it cease?

Transition Living
2: Source not symbol
1 Samuel 4–7

What do you think of when you think of the word 'Ark'? The Arc de Triomphe in Paris? HMS Ark Royal? Or maybe Noah's Ark? But do you ever think about the Ark of 1 Samuel – the Ark of the Covenant?

The Ark of the Covenant – a small box with cherub symbols on top and carried on two poles so that the four men with the job of transporting it could avoid touching it directly – was a very holy icon, a symbol of divine power. The Ten Commandments were in this box, as given to Moses on Mount Sinai, etched on tablets of stone. The Israelites carried the Ark around as a reminder to them that God was just and holy, that he had laws and values, and they as a people were bound by those laws and values.

Also in the Ark was manna, a reminder of God's provision. This was the strange food that God miraculously provided for them during their years of wandering in the wilderness. And there was at least one other thing in the Ark: Aaron's rod, the stick which had miraculously blossomed and was a sign of leadership.

At this point in the story Samuel is not a child anymore but a grown man. He's not only Eli's 'number two' but a significant prophetic voice in the nation. And the Israelites are at war with the Philistines – the brutal tribe who plagued them over many years.

In this particular battle (4:2) Israel is defeated by the Philistines, with about 4,000 of them lying dead on the battlefield. Defeated! And the Israelites' response is to bring out the Ark to see off the enemy (4:3). Here they are making the classic mistake of many religious groups – that of confusing a symbol of power with the power: God himself. They make an idol of a very important visual aid, thinking that the power resides in the Ark when actually,

> they are making the classic mistake of many religious groups – that of confusing a symbol of power with the power: God himself

although God occasionally endued the Ark with power, it is *God* who provides the power.

Almost all religious communities make this mistake, allowing some kind of idol to assume superstitious significance. Non-conformist churches are no more immune from this than those following liturgy. Churches which have no icons or statues may think they're beyond this, but actually they are in enormous danger of it! They fall into the trap of thinking that their style of music, or the organ, or the communion table take on holy icon-type significance. Actually, God is not in programme or structure. He might choose to bless it – and often does – but *he* is the one with whom we have relationship.

The children of Israel are fooled into believing that because they have the icon, they have the power; that because they have the symbol, they have the blessing of God. It's manifestly clear that they haven't, because they have been disobedient. But when the Ark arrives, along with Eli's two sons, a tremendous cheer goes up (4:5).

It's something like attitudes to national flags. Flags are so important to some people that they will die for them. But if a flag is captured or burned in an anti-government riot, it doesn't mean that the national power is weakened. So when the Ark of the Covenant is captured, does this mean that God's power is weakened? Of course not! But a superstitious people will behave as if it is. And this is what

happens: the Ark is captured, 30,000 Israelite soldiers lie dead, and that includes Eli's two sons (4:10,11).

Superstition is wrong thinking. Sometimes we expect divine protection because we say right things, do right things; because we're British or American or because we go to church. But the power is not in these symbols; it's in God and in a relationship with him. The Israelites had neglected that relationship and trusting in the symbol wasn't a substitute. The symbolic ending of the dynasty comes when Eli, hearing the news (4:18) falls off his judging chair and dies; and his daughter-in-law is shocked into premature labour and dies in childbirth (4:19). Her son is named Ichabod (4:21), reflecting the truth that 'the glory has departed' from Israel.

Likewise the glory of the western nations has departed. Materialism and selfishness has robbed us of our passion and wisdom. Honesty in public life is evaporating and truth disappearing from private life. Right living, right thinking and right speaking are no longer the common coinage. One of the western world's great visual aids, the twin towers of the World Trade Center in New York, was reduced to rubble on September 11, 2001 – a chilling wake-up call to a crumbling society.

Though the Ark is captured by the Philistines, though it is taken into the temple of a pagan god (5:2), we are reminded that God is not mocked. The next morning the

Materialism and selfishness
has robbed us of our passion and wisdom

Honesty in public life is evaporating and truth disappearing from private life

Global history is not settled by coalitions of western forces against terrorists or by any numbers of weapons of mass destruction

statue of the god Dagon is lying flat before the Ark (5:3) and the next day he's flattened again, this time headless and handless, in an attitude of worship (5:4)! The Philistines are overtaken with sickness (5:6). This all confirms the supreme power of God.

Global history is not settled by coalitions of western forces against terrorists or by any numbers of weapons of mass destruction. Though these things may happen, God is ultimately in control of human history. Eventually all will bow the knee to his Son, Jesus Christ.

The Philistines' elaborate procedures to get rid of the Ark of the Covenant that has brought them so much ill fortune are described in chapter 6. They recognise that they've done wrong to capture it and send it home with payment in gold. That's a picture of salvation. You turn your back on what's wrong and start again. But the difference is that we don't pay the price – Jesus has already done that, if we surrender to him! God accepts the payment Jesus has made by his death on the cross and we are saved. May God help us to go out into our culture with the salvation package: to say 'Your gods – materialism or folk religion or whatever – are false and won't sustain you! But God in Jesus Christ has paid the price and we can be set free and God's anger appeased, with freedom as the result.'

In chapter 7 Samuel again emerges onto the scene: Eli is dead; a new dynasty has arisen. The people have learned the lesson (7:2) that they should look to the Lord and not the Ark, the source and not the symbol.

Samuel is a very gifted leader. Knowing the Israelites' history of whingeing ingratitude, he sets up a memorial stone (7:12) – a monument to remind everyone that God has helped them. Perhaps if you're someone with a short memory and a tendency to moan, you too need to set up a memorial as a constant reminder of God's help. It could be a small pebble you carry in your pocket or put on the mantelpiece. Feel it or look at it in the midst of crisis and remember God's goodness, his generosity and his past help.

Transition Living Worksheet

2: Source not symbol

1 Samuel 4–7

1 What does 1 Samuel 4:3 show us about human nature?

_____

_____

• Why do we tend to blame God when we suffer?

_____

_____

• What was the real reason behind such a comprehensive defeat?

_____

_____

2 What indications are there that faith in God had degenerated into a kind of 'touch wood' superstition?

_____

_____

• In what ways is this true of our culture today?

_____

_____

3 Notice (4:7) how far God's reputation had travelled. Have you found that people know much about God?

_____

_____

• Is this helpful or unhelpful when it comes to sharing the gospel with them?

_____

_____

4 List the ways in chapter 5 that God's honour was defended.

_____

_____

• Do you find this part of the story alarming or reassuring?

_____

_____

5 How good is your memory? Do you need some kind of memorial stone (7:12) to remind you how good God has been to you? List some of his blessings to you, share them with the group, and express your praise in prayers of thanksgiving.

_____

_____

_____

Transition Living

3: Bad decisions made good

1 Samuel 8–12

As we travel through the highlights of Samuel's life we find that by the time we reach 1 Samuel chapter 8 he is an older man, appointing his own two oldest sons as judges for Israel, serving in the furthest corners of the kingdom.

But we read (8:3) that his sons are dishonest, accepting bribes and perverting justice. Isn't it fascinating that this is a re-run of the problem with Eli's sons? Eli is a weak and pathetic man and he has evil sons. Samuel is a godly, upright man – and he has evil sons! Tragic but true. What can we learn from this? That there are no guarantees! Every believing parent and grandparent wants their children and grandchildren to discover the faith they have. But every church has people who are deeply disappointed with the way their children have turned out, and cannot understand why they do not walk in the ways of the Lord. We need to think carefully about what we are investing in our children, at the same time recognising that when a child is old enough to choose, his destiny is in his own hands and he is responsible for those decisions. So it's not necessarily our fault if our child turns out bad. We shouldn't spend our lives agonising and feeling false guilt over our children's decisions.

> when a child is old enough to choose, his destiny is in his own hands and he is responsible for those decisions

The people ask Samuel to appoint a king (8:5). 'Samuel, you're getting old, and your kids are a disgrace! We certainly don't want them ruling over us!' That's an understandable motivation. The hereditary principle has never been a good one on which to base the leading of nations. Any nation in the world with a dictator who wants to pass power to his son, and then to *his* sons, is a nation which, within three generations, is terminally corrupt. That's why liberal democracy has evolved. Democracy is not an efficient form of government. The most efficient form of government is dictatorship: things get done, they get done now, and they get done in the way the dictator wants! Efficient – but dangerous!

But alongside that good motivation, the people want, symbolically, to oust the King of Heaven, Yahweh, the King of Israel, and produce their own human king. After 40 years of wilderness wandering, and the ups and downs of the judges, their cry is, 'God, help us to be like the other nations'. The pressure to conform is overwhelming.

I don't think there is a single person who does not feel at times the pressure to conform with those around them. There's pressure to take drugs or drink, or sleep around. But more subtle is the pressure to absorb other people's values

motivation, God does not leave them to their own devices. He gives them Saul, and although Saul degenerates as his life goes on, at this stage he is a humble man who wants to serve God.

That's an encouragement to anyone who knows they've made bad or stupid decisions which may have cost them dear. Of course there are consequences, but God can take bad decisions and turn them into good by his grace. He does not abandon us. He turns ugliness into beauty. Even though he might be utterly exasperated by the rebellion of the Israelites, he gives them better than they deserve.

When Saul becomes king, he meets significant challenges and in order to face them he needs to be **equipped** and **affirmed**.

He can succeed in his leadership because he is **equipped** by the anointing of the Spirit of God (10:1). Saul will be 'changed into a different person' (10:6). Samuel says he will

God can take bad decisions and turn them into good by his grace

such as materialism, because you don't want to be thought of as 'odd'. God wants to give us the power to be different; the power not to conform to others; the power of the Spirit to live conforming to God's will.

So the Israelites' request displeases Samuel and it's salutary to see his mature response: he prays about it (8:6). Samuel doesn't think that having a king will solve all their problems. And neither does God, who sees their request as evidence of their rejection of him. But they are insistent that having a king, like other nations, will solve everything. Finally God agrees, telling Samuel to let them have their way (8:21,22).

So that brings us to Saul, a tall young man, shy and embarrassed, but chosen by God. What's fascinating is that though the children of Israel make a bad choice with bad

prophesy, too. But that's not the *primary* evidence of God's Spirit at work – it's a changed life. Spiritual gift without spiritual character is not enough.

Saul is also **affirmed** for leadership (10:23,24). Remember that Samuel hadn't wanted a king. But here he is, generously affirming him before the people. Many Christian leaders are failing not because of a lack of anointing, but because of a lack of affirmation from God's people. So often churches chew leaders up and spit them out, leaving their lives a wreckage on the highway of Christian life. Affirmation, of course, can include correction and rebuke – that's often perfectly appropriate – but positive encouragement is vital.

Saul is challenged by having to face trouble-makers – people who don't want him. The tragedy is that this

Don't we look for things to cling to when the ship's going down?

haunted Saul throughout his kingship, and eventually he bought into their manipulation and jealousy.

Why do leaders need the equipping of the Spirit in incredible ways in their lives? Why do they need the affirmation of God's people? Because they are going to face opposition and difficulty.

So the people get their king. And, as in all times of significant national or international events, the people look to their leader for direction. Often that results in a keynote speech that impacts the leader's political career. And so, in chapter 12, Samuel is about to make the speech of his life.

This is a crucial point in the nation's history. There have been great celebrations over Saul's coronation. The people have got what they wanted! Theocracy is gone and monarchy is established. And so Samuel steps forward to speak. He begins by establishing that he is not like all the rest –

he dares to be different (12:3). He demonstrates that he is utterly accountable. He's leaving a standard of integrity against which all other leaders could be measured.

Secondly, Samuel gives them a lesson in history (12:6-13). They need it because they forget – like we forget so easily what God has done for us. He reminds them that Israel's leader has always been Jehovah, even though they have not always acknowledged him. Feeling vulnerable and insecure, they want to be like other nations that seem stronger and more powerful. They have forgotten the covenant promises of his awesome power and love (12:7). He takes them back to the Exodus, the greatest act of deliverance in Israel's history. They have forgotten the great things God had done.

Are we so different? When things get tough, when suffering comes, when the unpredictable and the unthinkable happen, are we so different? Don't we look out for earthly things that can be our defence mechanisms and our support systems? Don't we look for things to cling to when the ship's going down? So Samuel reminds them of their inconstancy, of the cycle of repentance and rebellion that has been repeated in their history.

That sad cycle occurs because of the reliance on rules as unconnected to relationship. When you move away from a relationship, you don't see the relevance of the rules. So you break the rules and then complain, 'Why wasn't God there to save me?'

great sense of security and sense come from knowing the God

To underline Samuel's message, God sends thunder and rain (12:18). And it's significant how the people respond, asking Samuel to call on *his* God. He's not *their* God any more. They'd lost track of the covenant relationship – the warmth, the breadth, the length, the height and depth of the incredible relationship with Yahweh, their God.

What is the way forward? For good or ill, they've got a king. But God is gracious (12:20-22). If they will return to him, he will not abandon them. But they need to be whole-hearted. They need to move from self-rule to giving God everything.

When we forget *who* we are and *whose* we are, we start behaving as if there is no one to whom we are accountable, no one to whom we belong. Yet God made us with a need to belong. We have a need for security and for significance. And great sense of security and sense of identity come from knowing the God who is at the centre of all things.

Take a leap forward in time. Samuel could hardly have imagined how this devastating speech was to be fulfilled, not through any earthly leader, but through Jesus hundreds of years ahead. He could not have imagined Jesus with three disciples praying on a mountain (Luke 9:28). They had a vision of two giants in Old Testament history – Moses and Elijah. They were discussing the new exodus (Luke 9:31), the new 'way out' Jesus is going to open up – a way for men and women out of the bondage of sin, self-rule, self-dependence.

On that mountain Peter's attempt to make some kind of physical memorial is interrupted by God himself. 'This is my Son, whom I have chosen; listen to him' (Luke 9:35). A short speech – but it's a trumpet blast from the past! It's a trumpet blast from the Psalms (Psalm 2:6,7): 'I have installed my King on Zion, my holy hill.' It's a trumpet blast from Isaiah 42:1, 'Here is my servant, whom I uphold, my chosen one in whom I delight'. It's a trumpet blast from Deuteronomy 18:15: 'The Lord your God will raise up for you a prophet like me… listen to him'.

God is announcing something pivotal. This is the prophet, priest, and king, standing on the mountain. This is the God-Man who wants to rule our hearts. He wants to be our defence. He wants to be our shelter. He wants to be our Rock. He alone is our true security.

# of identity
who is at the centre of all things

Transition Living Worksheet

3: Bad decisions made good

1 Samuel 8–12

1 Think about the people clamouring for a king (8:5). Why do you think the Lord sometimes lets us have our own way, even though it may hurt us?

_____

_____

_____

2 In what ways do Christians fall prey to mirroring the culture of the day rather than being different? List some examples and share them.

_____

_____

_____

3 What challenges do the leaders of your church face?
 • Are they equipped and affirmed?
 • Are they facing a cost in leading others?

_____

_____

_____

4 When Saul is anointed (10:1), the people are called the Lord's 'inheritance'. What do you think this means?

_____

_____

 • Does this encourage you?

_____

_____

5 What evidence is there that the Holy Spirit had come on Saul?

_____

_____

 • What might we expect as the signs of anointing in a person's life today?

_____

_____

6 Check out 12:20–25. How helpful is this as a plan for moving forward out of past failure?

_____

_____

_____

7 Pray in the group about decisions you are facing as individuals or as a local church.

Transition Living

4: Character, character, character!

1 Samuel 16

After Saul, who? God's prophet Samuel is sent (16:1) on an assignment to anoint the next king of Israel.

He is directed to Bethlehem, where he meets the seven sons of Jesse and finds that God has not chosen any of them (16:10) – but the eighth and youngest, who was not considered a likely option and had been left out in the fields taking care of the sheep. Samuel himself had thought the eldest the most impressive-looking (16:6), but God instructs him, 'Do not consider his appearance or his height, for I have rejected him. The Lord does not look at the things man looks at. Man looks at the outward appearance, but the Lord looks at the heart' (16:7).

Let's have a bit of sympathy for the seven other guys, all with high hopes that they might be the next king! We've all had experiences of rejection like that – the failed job interview or exam, not being chosen for a sports team. The reality was that they are not God's choice for the job.

Quite likely they would have thought the choice of their youngest brother was surprising. You can imagine a healthy young man coming in (16:12), tanned from working in the fields, perhaps sporting designer stubble, and with a

definite rugged outdoors appeal. Don't imagine that David was unattractive on the outside. He wasn't the runt of the litter, he was probably a good-looking guy. The main point is that beyond the physical – the bronzed David – there is an inner reality that is of greater significance.

We must not assume from this story that the physical is unimportant – but only that it is *less* important.

> a healthy young man coming in, tanned from working in the fields, perhaps sporting designer stubble, and with a definite rugged outdoors appeal

In previous generations this story has tempted preachers to claim that women shouldn't wear make-up. Or that really ugly Christians were far more likely to be called into mission or other work. Or that we shouldn't bother with exercise. We need to get the balance right. It's perfectly appropriate to take some care about external appearance, while at the same time recognising that *inner* beauty is more important to God.

After Samuel has anointed David, we move into a part of the story which has perplexed theologians down the years. We read (16:14) that the Spirit of God has left Saul, and that he is tormented by an evil spirit from the Lord.

This does seem to go against everything we know about the way our God acts. When evil spirits or demonic forces are spoken about in the New Testament, it is almost always spirit beings that are in view. However, when evil spirits are mentioned in the Old Testament, it is extremely difficult to be sure what's being spoken about. Is this a demonic force, oppressing King Saul? Is it a psychiatric disorder? Is it psychological stress? Is it an oppression of some kind? We really don't know what's going on here. But the net result is that when Saul is in depressive mood, and David, as someone skilled at playing on the harp, plays for him (16:23), Saul would experience 'relief': 'he would feel better, and the evil spirit would leave him'.

Music can be mood-altering. Here, God takes young David's harp playing, and supernaturally uses it to subdue a very depressed ageing king. At least their relationship started out positively!

As we examine this story, let's look at the amazingly mature character of Samuel. Remember, Samuel did not want Saul to be king. And yet Samuel mourns for Saul (15:35) because he's been rejected as Israel's leader. It wasn't, 'I told you so!' Having seen God's anointing on Saul, he is mature enough to follow Saul's leadership and grieve at the loss to the nation, despite the fact that this was not his personal choice. What remarkable maturity! Can you follow someone you personally don't like, but who God has put in place?

The church would be radically different if it were filled with people of this kind of maturity. In contrast, most of us are whimsical, moody, and infantile in our responses to these issues. There's deep immaturity about the way we react when circumstances don't go our way.

Another reason to wonder at Samuel's greatness is that he knew the fear of the Lord. Look at the response from the elders when he arrived in Bethlehem (16:4). They tremble. They're terrified of him because one of the local leaders had been put to death by Samuel for rebelling against Saul (15:33). The Bethlehem elders are wondering who's next on Samuel's hit list.

My cry to God is for men and women in leadership in the church and in our nation who are like Samuel. Our churches are sometimes led by people who are gifted administratively and pastorally – and those things are essential – but they don't have the breath of God about their beings. There is no fear of the Lord, there's no sense of his presence with them. Their sermons may be carefully crafted, their services lively, their administration carefully constructed – but where is the fear of God in it all? Christian leaders ought to be so close to God that they absolutely reek of his righteousness! And there is fear in their presence – not because they are intimidating as personalities, but because through them God shines his light and everyone knows that they will confront sin - however costly it is to them personally.

Those God anoints and appoints, he also equips. That means that as we pray for our leaders to be anointed and we pray for them to be appointed as people with godly character, we also pray for them to be properly equipped. What training can we offer to our home group leaders, to our Sunday School teachers, to our worship leaders? We need to excel in all that we give to God.

Some of us
are busy revising

Eventually the process of choosing a king takes place, the sacrifice is prepared and Jesse's sons are paraded before him. David has God's anointing, God's appointing, and God's equipping. If you look (16:3,6,13) you see the word 'anointing' repeated. Anointing was a physical act symbolising a spiritual act, and the spiritual act is spelt out in verse 13:

we men and women who are right with God? Are we – from the inside – serving him and following him? Some of us will find ourselves facing God one day, having fooled people for years because inside there's a vacuum where there should be a godly, holy, beating heart.

> ## Some of us will find ourselves facing God one day, having fooled people for years because inside there's a vacuum where there should be a godly, holy, beating heart.

'from that day on the Spirit of the Lord came upon David in power'. The physical anointing from the horn of oil is symbolic of the anointing of the Spirit for kingship so that David could rule the nation with authority. The prophets' horns would quite likely have been fairly large and full of a thick treacly substance, much thicker than olive oil. When we pray for healing for people today we tend to take a small amount of oil and do a little cross very delicately on their foreheads – we don't want to mess their hair up! But it was unlikely that in David's day this was just a little dribble, but a mega amount – a dramatic representation of the Holy Spirit releasing someone into leadership.

We need to pray for our leaders of every kind that there is an anointing on what they do. As a preacher I do not want to be the craftsman of a clever sermon, rather I want to be the deliverer of an anointed message. Anointing on many levels is what is needed to deliver us from sheer mediocrity.

The key to dynamic Christian leadership is always 'character, character, character'. It's what's going on inside us that is so fundamental. We might display all sorts of skills; we might be persuasive as orators; we might be attractive as leaders; we might be wise as strategic thinkers. But are

In the press there was a story about a secondary school where the English 'A' level students had studied Shakespeare's *Hamlet*. When they came to the examination room and the invigilator called for quiet, they turned their papers over to discover that the questions were all about Shakespeare's *The Tempest*. It was the correct paper, but the students were totally unprepared. The school had simply not paid attention to a change in the curriculum.

Some of us are busy revising 'materialism' and we're going to be examined on 'Jesus'! Some of us, despite all we display to others, are not walking with integrity before the Lord. God sees what's inside. It is a tragedy of enormous proportions when our whole life is an act which our inner life denies.

If we're living a lie, what should we do? Abandon coming to church, because we're just faking it? No – the opposite! We should come with the intention of making what's externally true, internally true.

'materialism'
and we're going to be examined on 'Jesus'!

Transition Living Worksheet

4: Character, character, character!

1 Samuel 16

1 How much are your assessments of others affected by the external?

_____

_____

• What could we do to change our inclination to make judgements based on external appearances?

_____

_____

2 Have you ever had to work under the authority of someone you really disliked?

_____

_____

• How well did you cope?

_____

_____

• What did you learn?

_____

_____

3 Have you ever been under the leadership of someone you felt was 'God-anointed'?

_____

_____

• How was that demonstrated?

_____

_____

4 Saul was tormented by 'an evil spirit from God'.
• Did God engineer this or simply allow it?

_____

_____

_____

5 Has God ever shown you that you were spending too much effort on something relatively irrelevant – that you were revising _Hamlet_ when the exam was going to be on _The Tempest?_ Share your experiences in the group.

_____

_____

_____

6 Has Samuel 16 shown you anything valuable about a) praying for and b) supporting those in leadership in both the national and local church? Spend some time praying for your leaders as a group now.

Transition Living
5: Power encounter

1 Samuel 17

The story of David and Goliath is a source of tremendous encouragement – because it's a story that affirms that whatever giants we are facing in life, there is victory with God!

The Philistines were classic enemies of the Jews, and had been for a long time. This is showdown time! We're in a valley. On one side (17:3), occupying the high ground, is the Israelite army. On the other side are the Philistines. And in between is an enormous valley which is a kind of 'no man's land'. In any military battle you want to be on the hilltop, not in the valley below. So neither of these two military forces wanted to leave their high vantage place to come down into the valley *first*, so giving an advantage to the opposition, who could then throw arrows and spears at them from above. It was a standoff; a stalemate.

Goliath, for the Philistines, stands on an escarpment and can be heard shouting across the echoing valley (17:8). The Bible says he was over nine feet tall. Some people speculate that this was an example of the medical condition of 'giantism'. Interestingly, people who are excessively tall often don't live into old age because their bones are weak, easily broken or malformed. Perhaps this is why David's stone was able to penetrate Goliath's forehead so easily. We don't know the truth of that idea. However, even if Goliath wasn't weak-boned, he was possibly weak-brained, because he certainly didn't anticipate the problem.

The giant was wearing a huge amount of bronze armour, weighing over 100 pounds (17:5). And his bronze spear, though state of the art, was also extremely heavy. So this man is not only huge, but he's very strong.

Goliath issues a challenge to settle the outcome (17:8-10). This was not an unusual way of settling a dispute in those days and actually quite utilitarian, as it meant that though a whole nation might come under slavery at least it wasn't completely wiped out.

We read that everyone is 'dismayed and terrified' (17:11) – including Saul. We already know that Saul is a taller-than-average guy, so perhaps the expectation is that he is the right man to take on the giant Goliath.

> it's a story that affirms that whatever giants we are facing in life, there is victory with God!

The challenge remains uncontested for 40 days. But meanwhile (17:12) enter the hero! David finds himself near enough to the front line to hear the regular challenge, and discovers that Saul has promised status, wealth, and power through marriage to his own daughter to the person who defeats Goliath. What's more, the victor will never pay tax again for the rest of his life (17:25)!

David has a meeting with Saul in which he offers to take on the giant (17:32). Despite Saul's ridiculing, David feels that defending his sheep against lions and bears has prepared him pretty well for such a fight. He rejects the offer of armour and goes out to take on Goliath, who is annoyed and angry at being made to fight a boy. The slingshot does its worst. Goliath dies, and the Philistines flee in complete disarray, pursued at pace by the Israelites (17:52).

The problems we face are sometimes as enormous and intimidating as Goliath. They can be huge obstacles to our spiritual progress. It's very dangerous to say, 'Come to Jesus, and your problems will be solved!' For many of us, coming to Jesus is when our problems *begin*, because we

us. The church is being mocked, labelled unimportant, devalued, ignored, oppressed, sidelined.

David (17:26) is the first person to see the spiritual dimension of the problem with Goliath. It's not simply a military encounter. If the Philistine had won, their god Dagon would have been imposed on the Israelites – so it would have been a religious defeat as much as a military one. David sees that God's honour is at stake. It's a clash of ideologies. Not just the Philistines against the Israelites. But Dagon versus God.

We face similar clashes today – with other ideologies and other morality systems. Though, for example, ordinary Muslim men and women must be treated with dignity, love, and respect, the ideology which lies behind Islam has devilish and demonic implications which directly oppose our God. There are New Age influences out there. There are occultic superstitions prevalent in our society. There is pornography polluting minds and hearts. There is abuse of the poor. There are all kinds of Goliath ideologies actively opposing the church. That's why prayer is so

For many of us, coming to Jesus is when our problems begin, because we then have all the spiritual forces of darkness arrayed against us

then have all the spiritual forces of darkness arrayed against us. Not only do we have all the usual problems that every human being has: worries about the family, health, finance, etc. But, because we are believers, we find ourselves in spiritual warfare. Being a Christian is about having the power of Jesus in our lives - but let's not underestimate the problems to be faced internally and externally.

Look at the word 'defy' which recurs (17:10,25) in this chapter. Goliath sets himself against the people of God. Similarly, the church is being defied in our day. Our nation's stand on sexuality, on honesty, on so many things, is against

important, because this is bigger than us! Unless we are prayerful, we'll never understand the forces ranged against us. We're in a spiritual battle for the honour of the living God.

Let's look at two key principles for defeating giants:

God uses weakness

David is so weak in comparison to Goliath. A boy against a man. A shepherd against a military man. But he wins because he's on God's side. God takes weak people and transforms the world – just as well, because otherwise the church would have to recruit the greatest intellects, the richest people, the people with the most influence, and only then would we have a chance of turning the world round.

Over a hundred years ago a young woman nicknamed the 'London Sparrow', a domestic servant called Gladys Aylward, saved up her money over years in order to buy a one-way ticket from Waterloo Station to China. Madness! She had to stop half-way across China because there was a war going on and everybody, including the driver, got off the train, and she had to walk 30 miles back through the snow to the nearest station until the next train came along. Staggering! This apparently weak little woman transformed huge parts of China by her Christian witness and her love.

David has been faithful in small things as a shepherd (17:34–37) so God gives him the opportunity to be faithful in big things. He has taken care of his father's sheep, defending them against lions – and those would be Asiatic lions, smaller than the African lions that we picture with huge manes. He's defended them against bears – again, not the big grizzlies but smaller bears common in that area. And, in defending his flocks, David grew up with a real sense of responsibility.

God has different methods

Saul dresses David in his own tunic and tries to give him armour which certainly doesn't fit (17:38,39). David in Saul's armour has become a kind of cliché for trying to do things you are not equipped to do. God's method is to take us as we are and to use us for his kingdom purpose, without pretence. We're not to pretend to be something we're not in order for God to use us. Sometimes we're tempted to ape certain styles of Christian leadership that we see, but God wants to use us just as we are, dedicated to him.

The Philistine giant comes against David with state-of-the-art technology: the very best in bronze weaponry. David definitely has the old technology: a leather sling and a few stones (17:40). It would be like standing up to a Cruise missile with a rifle! Except that David has come 'in the name of the LORD Almighty' (17:45), the name that Goliath has defied. Although God chooses to use the sling,

... a leather sling and a few stones. It would be like standing up to a Cruise missile with a rifle!

it's really irrelevant. David knows that the demise of the giant is guaranteed because the battle is not physical but spiritual.

Whatever giants we face today, we do so in the power of the One who can defeat the best weaponry with a sling and stone. Our problems are his problems. Our battle is his battle. Though we are pathetically weak, he is strong. When we open our eyes to see beyond the physical problem to the spiritual power of God, our prayer changes. We can implore the armies of the King of Kings with confidence to act on our behalf to defeat the giants we face – whether they are personal, national or international. A victorious Christian life is not a superior brand of Christianity reserved for the elite of the elect. It is the normal Christian life for every believer.

Transition Living Worksheet

5: Power encounter
1 Samuel 17

1 What was at stake for Israel when Goliath made his challenge?

_____

_____

• What threats of similar proportions are facing our country today?

_____

_____

• What principles from this story would help us tackle them?

_____

_____

2 Why was David both an unlikely and yet a perfect candidate?

_____

_____

_____

3 What personal lessons can you draw from this power encounter that will help you in your daily life?

_____

_____

_____

4 Do you readily recognise the spiritual dimensions to problems?

_____

• What are the advantages of doing this?

_____

_____

• Possible disadvantages?

_____

_____

5 Discuss: 'All God's giants have been weak men [and women] who did great things for God because they reckoned on his being with them' (missionary pioneer Hudson Taylor).

_____

_____

_____

6 'A victorious Christian life is not a superior brand of Christianity reserved for the elite of the elect. It is the normal Christian life for every believer.' Do you agree?

_____

_____

_____

7 Share in the group about any giants you are facing right now and pray for one another.

Transition Living
6: Downward spiral
1 Samuel 18

After a promising start, we find King Saul on a downward spiral. His story becomes a sorry tale of jealousy, fear, manipulation, lying, obsession, and murder plots!

Naturally everyone is celebrating because David has defeated Goliath. They sing his praises – and Saul is angry. There's a lovely little Hebrew phrase which is a classic Old Testament understatement, 'this refrain galled him' (18:8). He was livid with jealousy!

Think about a similar situation in church life. 'Housegroup leader A has attracted 10 people to their group, but leader B has 20 people – hasn't she done well!' Or, 'Evangelist C has seen hundreds coming to faith – but evangelist D has thousands making decisions!'

The fault line of jealousy in Saul's character leads to complete and dramatic character decay. Unquestionably, when we are jealous or envious there is a crack that allows Satan in. And this is particularly true in leadership.

I remember listening to a discussion on the radio on 'Why do people hate footballer superstar David Beckham?' Taking part was someone who purported to be a professor in football studies and a woman who had written a poem about David Beckham. I found it pretentious nonsense from beginning to end! To me, the answer to the question is obvious. Though widely idolised, there are many people who hate David Beckham because he's talented, he's got a gorgeous wife and tons of cash! After 20 minutes the discussion *finally* touched on jealousy, and they agreed that it might be a factor. We look at someone like David Beckham or other sporting idols or celebrities and think to ourselves, 'He earns all that money just by kicking a football around. What I do is far more important. Why am I not earning all this money? And why doesn't my wife look like her!' It's jealousy!

> There are many people who hate David Beckham because he's talented, he's got a gorgeous wife and tons of cash!

Perhaps you're at school or college studying hard for your exams. You start thinking, 'Why is it that I work my socks off to pass exams and still don't do very well, and so-and-so in the corner there plays about in lessons, hardly seems to concentrate and they get fantastic marks!' We're envious of their intellectual ability.

Or we're jealous of someone else's easy life: 'Why is it that I'm ill so often, or depressed, or struggling? Look at them, with their perfect family and everything working smoothly!'

So jealousy creeps in to every area of our lives, rendering us ineffective as believers and ineffective as leaders. We get so consumed with wanting what someone else has that our focus is radically shifted away from discipleship.

Jealousy is the fissure in the soul which allows the devil in to wreck Saul's life. He starts so well (9:2): head and shoulders above everybody else, a prophet, a really great guy!

The lesson for us is that we need to check that we are not getting jealous because someone is preferred over us, or because someone has got results or status or public appreciation when we think *we* deserve it. One sign of maturity is to be able to affirm a rival. Envy should be so dead in us that we are satisfied by who we are in God.

Saul is deeply unsatisfied. He cannot keep his jealous eyes off David and longs to do him down. Jealousy leads to fear (18:12,29) because he feels his position is threatened. We all know that feeling, don't we? Someone turns up at your place of work and they are on the same management level that you are. They are spectacularly successful, innovative and creative and everybody's talking about their department. Isn't it easy to fear, 'What's going to happen to *me*?

What's going to happen to *my* department? What's going to happen to *my* budget? What's going to happen to *my* career opportunities?'

Or someone moves into the church who sings or plays a musical instrument better, who leads better, or is gifted with children or young people. Our defence mechanisms are raised, and our envy of their gifts makes us afraid.

So when Saul looks as if he is just fulfilling his promise (18:17) in rewarding David, his hidden agenda is to raise David to the heights of responsibility where he'll be at greater risk of being killed in battle. Jealousy leads to fear and fear leads to manipulation. Saul's manipulation is so horrible that he even uses his own daughter in his evil plans (18:21). Micah is part of the snare to trap David into an untimely death.

Perhaps we think we wouldn't be so manipulative. But that may be because we simply don't have the power that Saul has! Some of us aren't that creative in sinning simply because we don't have much power. But we're not, for example, above a bit of creative gossip to destroy someone's reputation.

Saul's manipulation leads to lying (19:6). David won't be put to death, he assures his son Jonathan, and takes an oath on it. But it's a lie. He's on a downward spiral that began with his jealousy. Very soon this becomes obsessive to the point where he himself pins David against the wall with his spear (18:10,11). This is no accident, but part of his determination to remove David as a rival for the throne.

Let's not pretend that we might not descend to the same depths if we had the opportunity and the power that Saul had. Our own revenge is kept within limits because we lack

What we're wanting needs to be

Our souls will be satisfied when

not the

the power. But God wants us to act with grace towards those who might so easily be the objects of our envy.

If anyone has reason to be jealous of David it is Jonathan, the natural successor to Saul's throne. But Jonathan and David are firm friends and Jonathan acts with dignity and compassion throughout. Jonathan is content with what God has called him to, content with what God has given him, so that he is able to affirm his rival.

Jealousy needs to be nipped in the bud, given to God as soon as it arises. We need to feel secure in God, assured of our self-worth, knowing that we are loved and known by him. Then we won't be constantly wanting what others have to the point of being distracted from the things of eternity. What we're wanting needs to be what God wants to give us. Our souls will be satisfied when they are filled with God's stuff, not the stuff we might want to cram them with. So often Christians are dissatisfied, and it's because on the one hand they want to follow Jesus, and on the other they want to hang onto their envy and jealousy of others. God wants to satisfy us with himself, and God is the only true satisfaction for us.

The episode where David escapes from Saul while his wife Micah fools everyone into thinking that David's in bed (19:11–17) is the stuff of Hollywood movies. David runs off to Samuel. This is followed by a very bizarre sequence of events (19:18–24) when everyone seems to be prophesying under the influence of the Spirit of God. Somehow God's Spirit is so powerful that even the soldiers sent to capture David are sucked into a worship experience. Even more fantastic, a second group turn up and they, too, are overwhelmed by the Spirit. And a third group! And then even Saul himself! What does this tells us? It tells us that despite the fact that God gives you and me the dignity and the freedom of free will so that our decisions actually

Envy should be so dead in us that we are satisfied by who we are in God

change things and shape the world, in the end God's plan will not be thwarted and God's purposes will be worked out. God's plan is that David should be the next king, and no human power or hellish power is going to stop that happening.

Likewise, even though we have complete freedom, the destiny of our planet is not in doubt. The Spirit of God will not allow men or nations or spirit forces or anything to determine the destiny of our planet. Jesus is coming back, and no force on earth can alter that timetable. God is in control.

what God wants to give us.
they are filled with God's stuff,
stuff we might want to cram them with

Transition Living Worksheet

6: Downward spiral

1 Samuel 18

1   David comes off well in this story. But is there another part of his life in which he demonstrates the same manipulative jealousy as Saul does?

_____

_____

_____

2   In which area of your life do you find yourself most susceptible to jealousy: within the family/ at school or college/ your place of work/ in the church?

_____

_____

_____

3   How can we affirm those with superior gifting/ abilities to ourselves?

_____

_____

•   Is there some positive affirmation/ encouragement you could give someone this coming week?

_____

_____

4   Has there been a Jonathan in your life who has affirmed and encouraged you, even though it meant loss for them? Share your experiences.

_____

_____

_____

5   Do you feel loved and valued by God all the time/ sometimes/ hardly ever/ never? Share your feelings with the group.

_____

_____

_____

6   What gifts would make this group/ your local church, more effective for the kingdom of God?

_____

_____

•   Spend some time praying as a group that God-given and God-glorifying gifts will be released within yourselves and within the wider church.

Transition Living
7: True friendship
1 Samuel 20

Our culture struggles to make commitment to long-lasting, loyal and meaningful relationships. And the story of David and Jonathan provides us with some significant principles about making and keeping friends.

Western society in the third millennium is not good at friendship. Marriage itself, for example, is a key area of friendship under threat. Many people, particularly those in the public arena, don't bother to get married at all or not until a baby is on the way when they feel that marriage might be a nice, sentimental thing to do. And many marriages end in separation and divorce. We see people in *Hello!* magazine on their third, fourth or fifth marriage, and somehow it's portrayed as being attractive and glamorous. We live in an age of the disposable, so if the relationship doesn't work out we can junk it and get another one tomorrow. Sadly, so many of the celebrities we see on our TV screens die lonely, disappointed and bitter people. The way they treat their marriages is the way they treat the more everyday relationships of life. Often they have no one around in their old age who has known them for more than a few years. Many of them are alienated from their partners, cut off from their children and condemned to a superficiality of relationships in which there is no emotional sustenance.

David goes to Jonathan for some understanding of how he is being treated by Saul (20:1). They hatch an incredible plot (20:5). David is due at a feast at the palace and he says, 'Look, Jonathan, if I don't turn up I'll probably be missed, so let's use that situation to get an indication of what real my standing is with your dad'. And they come up with a code of shooting arrows to communicate Saul's real feelings towards David.

Predictably, Saul's anger flares up at the feast, Jonathan discovers the real extent of his father's feelings against David,

> We live in an age of the disposable, so if the relationship doesn't work out we can junk it and get another one tomorrow

and the arrow communication is deployed. David and Jonathan exchange a few moments of friendship before David flees.

Saul and Jonathan have a major relationship failure. Notice that Jonathan is quite clear about his father. He doesn't let filial ties blind him to the fact that Saul has lost the plot spiritually (20:13). Saul had once been walking close to God. He was numbered with the prophets. He was a significant person, God's choice to be the first king of Israel – but now he's a 'has-been' spiritually. The past was glorious, the present is disappointing, and the future looks even worse.

The challenge for us is that our relationships with one another start to go pear-shaped when our relationship with God becomes flawed. As Christians, our relationships with friends, husbands, wives or children can't happen irrespective of our relationship with God. When we want to rescue a friendship under pressure we need first to go to God, asking for forgiveness, and then go to the person to ask for forgiveness.

In Psalm 51 David talks about his flawed relationship with Bathsheba, recognising that he has sinned against God and he needs to get right with God if he wants to be right with others. Saul is in bad shape because he is no longer right with God and so all his relationships are screwed up (20:30–34). Notice that he can't even refer to Jonathan's mother or David by name. This is a complete family breakdown, which has its climax in attempted murder (20:33).

We all need to be in a place of strong and good friendships, whether we are talking about friendship in the context of marriage, relationships with children, or with other people. Our society desperately needs models of good friendship. There is a great deal of loneliness in our society and we're not just talking about elderly or single parents living alone.

We are talking about a lonely ache in the souls of today's men and women of all ages and situations.

Before we go further let's face up to the contention made in a sizeable body of literature in the last 20 years asserting that David and Jonathan were 'gay', that what the Bible describes here is a homosexual relationship. Those promoting this draw attention to 20:17 and 20:41 for example. Even more damning, from the liberal viewpoint, is 2 Samuel 1:26 where David laments Jonathan's death saying, 'Your love for me was wonderful, more wonderful than that of women'.

Our culture looks on same-sex relationships with some approval. This is not to say that the majority of people in Britain view same-sex relationships with approval, but that the opinion-formers – particularly those in the media – view it with approval.

Straightforward Biblical exposition at this point will lead us to a completely different conclusion. The attempt to foist onto this passage a third millennium model of relationships is a grotesque distortion of the Bible, and a horrifyingly naïve misreading of Old Testament culture. Men in the Middle East kiss each other regularly. The kiss on both cheeks is part of the cultural exchange. There is nothing 'gay' about it. It is the norm for men in the Middle East, in Africa, in Asia, to hold hands or walk arm in arm.

In the West we have our own cultural norms in terms of expressing friendship. For example, if you go out in a group to a restaurant it doesn't seem possible for the women in the group to go to the washroom on their own; they seem to have to go with a friend for some reason! Men tend not to need other men to accompany them to the washroom! Men and women are different, and behave differently in different cultures.

it would be a grotesque
anything here other than the
which is **wholesome** and

Even in the church we operate different norms. Outside the church there is a lot of respect for people's personal space. On a train, people choose to sit as far away from others as they can. In the rush hour, where proximity is inevitable, people avoid eye contact. But within the church family we react in a different and more affectionate way. It's OK for even grown men to hug each other in public. This is not inappropriate; there's nothing sexual in it. This kind of love is part of our liberation as Christians, and of course we need to take care not to overstep the boundaries. But it is part of evangelical culture – although it can seem very odd to people outside the church.

In the same way the love between Jonathan and David was culturally appropriate and *not* a reflection of their sexuality. Blurring between genders is a big issue in our world, and some use Bible passages such as these for their own agendas. The biblical view is clear: homosexual genital activity is forbidden by Scripture and must be rejected as wrong, but homosexual people are loved by God. Many with homosexual orientation choose to be celibate. Those that don't must be received, accepted and loved in the same way as those who have broken any of God's laws. There's no place in the church for homophobic behaviour. Loving the sinner and hating the sin still remains God's policy.

So it would be a grotesque misreading of these passages to see anything here other than the deepest male-bonding friendship which is wholesome and without a shred of sexual innuendo. Indeed, it's based on five principles which represent real guidelines on friendship which are relevant to us today.

Firstly, true friendship is **established on commitment**, as are all really successful relationships. In 18:1-4 Jonathan gives David various personal items as a sign of a covenant between them – just like a couple exchange wedding rings as a sign of mutual commitment. A friendship with no

We are talking about a lonely ache in the souls of today's men and women of all ages and situations

commitment soon runs out of steam. It is superficial, it will break easily. Many children and teens have life-long friendships that last a month! It's passing, transitory. And many people in our society have not matured beyond that. So we have marriages that are adolescent; they last a few months in terms of affection. You've got to *work* at it; there's got to be commitment. If I'm going to have a strong marriage or a strong friendship I'm going to stick with that person, and love them through thick and thin. If the friendship is nothing more than an annual Christmas letter, it might as well not exist. There has to be a real two-way commitment otherwise it's superficial and of no value.

Secondly, good friendship **copes with disagreement**. David and Jonathan have a disagreement (20:1–4) but their friendship copes. Within the Body of Christ we need each other, even if we have all kinds of disagreement about how the church should operate. Within marriage the same principle applies. It's hard to live in the same house over a period of time and agree about everything. People fall out over relatively trivial things – the design of the wallpaper or when to replace the car or the top being left off the toothpaste or the toilet seat being left up! – but the strong relationship will survive.

misreading of these passages to see deepest male-bonding friendship without a shred of sexual innuendo

Thirdly, good friendship is **based on truth**. Jonathan realises his friendship with David is based on the truth, not on sweeping things under the carpet. And it's truth beyond filial loyalty. Jonathan doesn't pretend truth is a lie just because his dad is in the frame, even though it's painful to him. There was no room for compromise in their strong friendship. Sometimes we suffer over the truth in our rela-

Let's ask God to deliver us from the flawed relationships which are epitomised by Saul's life, to help us build true friendships with people which can cope with disagreement, which are clearly covenanted together, which are loyal and which are founded in deep Christian love. May God forgive our superficiality. We want to have a deep abiding love for one another in the church, as well as in the community as

Our entire society is into loyalty deficit right now. Typically, we are loyal to a cause for as long as it suits our needs and then we abandon it

tionships. When our children or our friends have done something wrong, it breaks our hearts. But we have to recognise the truth even when it's painful.

Fourthly, good friendship is **secured by loyalty**. When Jonathan made a covenant commitment with David (20:16,17), he must have known he was cursing his own father. But the friendship mattered, and he was fiercely loyal. And loyalty is to be encouraged, in our families and in the church family. There must be loyalty to each other, to the mission of the church, to meeting together for worship and fellowship. Our entire society is into loyalty deficit right now. Typically, we are loyal to a cause for as long as it suits our needs and then we abandon it. We no longer feel the need to be loyal fans for a lifetime to the same football club – we change allegiance if they're doing badly. Loyalty is out, expediency is in! We need to stay loyal to our friendships even when it's not trendy or beneficial or easy. A true friend stays loyal through the storms.

Finally, true friendship is **sealed by genuine love**. When David weeps (20:41) perhaps it's because he realises how much loyalty is costing Jonathan. It meant Jonathan was never going to be king even though he should have been. He was never going to be honoured. He wasn't even going to live long. David wept at the measure of love which lays down life's ambitions for friendship. When I lay down my life so that my friends can succeed, that is true friendship and true love.

a whole – a love which forgives errors and mistakes; a love that can cope when we fall out; a love which washes over us and builds us into the people God wants us to be.

Transition Living Worksheet

7: True friendship
1 Samuel 20

1 'Our entire society is into loyalty deficit right now.' Do you agree or disagree?

_____

_____

_____

• What evidence can you put forward to support your viewpoint?

_____

_____

_____

2 Why do you think the flawed relationships of celebrities are idolised in our mass media?

_____

_____

_____

3 Have you experienced good role models of strong friendship in your life? Share your experiences.

_____

_____

_____

4 How did Jesus exemplify the very best in standards of friendship?

_____

_____

_____

5 What practical steps can we take to ensure the lonely do not remain lonely in our churches?

_____

_____

_____

6 Are any of your friendships being tested at present? (There's no need to share details, or name names.)

_____

_____

• How can you affirm your commitment to the other person?

_____

_____

• Are there any difficult truths that need facing?

_____

_____

7 Spend some time praying for each other's key relationships.

Transition Living
8: Resisting pressure
1 Samuel 24

Saul and David are larger-than-life characters. Saul is a giant of a king whose star is waning at this point in the story. And David, whose star is rising, is a giant of a man set to be king.

Their behaviour is totally opposite. One of them is acting honourably before God; the other is behaving obsessively and dishonourably.

In chapter 24 we find David in the En Gedi Desert, pursued by Saul. It's a pretty unpromising environment apart from the odd oasis – very rugged, a particularly uninviting wilderness. And, with disarming honesty, the Bible describes Saul going into a cave to relieve himself. However, don't imagine this is just a little cave. It is most likely that Saul is in the opening section of a massive underground network of caves, quite common in the Middle East. David and his men are actually 'far back in the cave' (24:3). They can't believe their luck – their arch enemy is actually delivering himself into their hands!

We read that David's response is to cut off a bit of Saul's robe. Sounds ridiculous, doesn't it? If I was in the men's loos and someone came up behind me and cut a bit off my coat, I'd notice, believe me! So is this just fabrication? Well, we need to remember that rulers in this time didn't exactly travel light. They moved around with endless suitcases in tow, lots of people carrying fruit and water and all sorts of things they needed. And they often travelled in robes of state, even wearing a crown. Saul was travelling in style with his 3000 'chosen men'. You can imagine him getting off his horse or camel and bundling up his enormous robe with its huge flowing train, gathering it all up and maybe throwing it up over his shoulder to try to get it out of the way so that he could relieve himself unencumbered. We're not talking about a simple shift or jacket, but massive royal

If I was in the men's loos and someone came up behind me and cut a bit off my coat, I'd notice, believe me! So is this just fabrication?

robes. Also, it's likely that David's eyes are used to the dark because he's been in the caves for a while, while Saul has come in from the bright sunshine and can see very little. So it's not that difficult for David to cut something – maybe a little tassel off the train – and retreat into the dark recesses of the cave.

But David feels guilty (24:5) and lets Saul go on his way. Then he confronts Saul with what he's done, trying to achieve reconciliation. This is an odd conversation without some understanding of the geography. It's likely David is calling down to Saul from a rocky clifftop into the valley. So, in terms of time, because of the steepness of the terrain they're probably quite far apart. But, in terms of distance, they're pretty close. David is at a safe vantage point and a conversation is quite possible. In their exchange Saul recognises David's honourable actions (24:19) and asks David to swear an oath that he will not harm him or his family.

Our newspapers are full of stories of people who are so angry and obsessive that they take someone else's life in a fit of rage. Some of us spend our lives thinking about how to get even with the boss or the company that's making life miserable for us. Some of us hate the man or woman we're married to because they've let us down, or hate our parents for the way they brought us up, or hate our children for not turning out the way we wanted them to. Some of us have been badly hurt – but if we continue to behave this way, it will kill *us*. We need to turn to God from our anguish, ask for forgiveness, and behave in new ways. We don't want to be Sauls – we want to be Davids!

David was behaving honourably, living in the light of the fact that one day he would be king; his behaviour today was shaped by what he was going to become tomorrow. You want to be a doctor? Then you study certain subjects to exam level, determined by that goal. Your behaviour now makes the future possible. Want to be a sportsman? You

Remorse is about emotion but repentance is about behaviour

Just a little while ago (22:17) Saul has been murdering innocent priests in his obsessive pursuit of David. He is utterly driven by his hatred and jealousy of David. And he's been neglecting his duty as king for the same reason (23:26,27). While he's pursuing David in the east, his land and people are being attacked by the Philistines from the west. His behaviour is characterised by remorse and not repentance. His response (24:16) sounds like repentance but it's not – because two chapters later he's trying to kill David again. Remorse is a great place to start, but it's different to repentance. In repentance we move from remorse to determination, with God's help, to turn our lives around and go in a different direction. Remorse is about emotion but repentance is about behaviour. Though Saul felt convicted about his sin in the emotion of the moment, he was not willing for a change in his behaviour.

train now with the aim of entering the Olympics or the World Cup in the future. If you're a Christian your future is determined already. Whether you've 40 minutes or 40 years left to live, you're going to be with God forever, and your behaviour now *must* be a preparation for that destiny.

That's why David could resist pressure from his peers (24:9,10) to kill Saul when he had the opportunity. The pressure from those around us to do the wrong thing can be enormous. Young people are under tremendous pressure from their peers at college; many people are under pressure from the anti-Christian values and ethos of their workplaces. That's why we need the power of the Spirit in us; that's why David needed to know he was God's man. We all conform unless there's a greater power within us to stand against the pressure.

David also respects authority (24:6,10). The Bible is very clear that authority is to be respected. It's a difficult balance, because the Bible also says we should oppose authority where it breaks God's laws, and Christians have been mar-

fun than hearing that someone who hurt you has been badly hurt themselves! But God tells us that vengeance is his.

Life has dealt some of us some very unfair blows, and it takes a lot not to adopt the world's values and reactions about our rights

tyred for their faith down 2000 years because they've said 'no' to the government, and 'yes' to God. Notice that there's real humility in David (24:14). He reminds Saul that he's as powerless as a flea and has no intention of taking his kingship by force. He's not going to take a shortcut to accomplish God's purposes; he's not looking for revenge; he is going to wait for God's timing. We all need to leave vengeance in God's hands. Life has dealt some of us some very unfair blows, and it takes a lot not to adopt the world's values and reactions about our rights. There's nothing more

God can help us to resist peer pressure and instead listen to his voice. Even when we feel justified in doing this or doing that, we need to listen closely enough to the Spirit to act as Jesus would have acted.

Transition Living Worksheet

8: Resisting pressure
1 Samuel 24

1 What do you think of David's attempt at reconciliation (24:9)?

_____

_____

• Can you identify areas in your community or church where reconciliation has been effective?

_____

_____

• Or areas where reconciliation is needed?

_____

_____

2 Will living today in the expectation of eternity make us 'too heavenly-minded to be any earthly use'?

_____

_____

• What changes of mindset might be needed to make us live with the perspective of eternity?

_____

_____

• What changes of behaviour?

_____

_____

3 What pressures to conform do you identify in our society at large?

_____

_____

• And in your own life?

_____

_____

• Are these pressures always negative?

_____

_____

4 'It's not fair!' Many people have a 'chip on their shoulder' about the unfair way they feel life has treated them. How do you respond when people talk in these terms?

_____

_____

5 Share within the group about pressure to conform that you are experiencing and pray for one another.

Transition Living
9: Descent into evil

1 Samuel 25–28

It's fascinating that most of the truth taught in the Bible is taught through stories. Huge parts of the Bible is story – true accounts of God's interaction with real people in real situations. Doctrine wrapped up in bodies.

And the ultimate example is, of course, Jesus. God doesn't so much *tell* us the truth about Jesus – he sends Jesus to *embody* the truth.

In this section of 1 Samuel, God is teaching us truth through the story of four lives: Nabal, Abigail, David and Saul.

Nabal is a man of mega wealth, but surly and mean; and he is married to Abigail, an intelligent and beautiful woman. David makes an approach to Nabal (25:4–8), asking for some sheep for himself and his band of 600 men to roast for a festival, on the grounds that they had left Nabal and his sheep alone to date, though other men living rough might have seen them as fair game. And David has actually looked after Nabal's people. He feels he's owed something and that, anyway, Nabal won't really miss a few sheep as he's so rich.

Is this a polite and reasonable approach? Or the opening gambit of some kind of protection racket, said in tones of menace? At least to begin with, I think it would have been a more gentle approach. But Nabal's response (25:10) suggests he is looking for excuses not to be generous – not a good reaction in a culture that prized hospitality highly. Requests for food, water and shelter were generally met willingly, even from complete strangers. Unsurprisingly, David and his men prepare for force. And word reaches

Is this a polite and reasonable approach? Or the opening gambit of some kind of protection racket, said in tones of menace?

Abigail's ears. Notice (25:14–17) that Nabal has lost the respect of his servants. They say he's a very wicked man – and they say it to his wife, which is pretty risky unless you feel she shares your view.

Abigail loses no time in preparing a serious feast (25:18). She rides out to David, greets him, and apparently describes her husband in very disloyal terms. Bear in mind that wives were collected in those days a little like cattle and she does not necessarily have deep affection for this man. Quite likely, as far as Nabal is concerned she is just another pretty face in his harem. Her insightful response to David instantly turns him back from his intention to slaughter everyone. Of course, David is influenced in this by the arrival of food as well as Abigail's sound arguments. He doesn't really want blood on his hands, particularly as a future king. It's quite likely, too, that he is susceptible to an attractive woman!

The next day (25:37) when Nabal is sobering up after a drunken feast Abigail tells him what has happened. Realising how close to death he has come, he seems to suffer a kind of heart attack or stroke. After ten days in some sort of coma, he dies – obviously a judgement from God. David is saved from the need to take revenge for Nabal's contempt. He promptly asks Abigail to marry him (25:39). This is not simply a very speedy courtship; there seems to have been some issue of protection going on here. Probably she would be disinherited or homeless as a result of Nabal's death. However, it's unlikely that David's motives were purely altruistic! In a sad little postscript (25:44), we hear that David's previous wife Michal had been given to someone else as a wife by Saul.

This husband and wife team of Nabal and Abigail are a reminder to us of how people can be very different although living in the same household. They are both religious Jews, but there isn't the heart commitment to God in Nabal that affects his lifestyle and character. He knows about God but he is greedy, ungrateful, ungenerous, proud and self-centred.

There are many today even within our churches with a head knowledge of God who haven't allowed it to change their

Religious observance is not enough; we have to bow the knee to God and become more like Jesus

lives. As well as a loyalty deficit in our society, we are suffering from a discipleship deficit in our churches. We need people who are determined not just to know *about* God but to let their lifestyles be determined by what God says and does. Religious observance is not enough; we have to bow the knee to God and become more like Jesus. We have to see the effects of knowledge lived out in behavioural change and character transformation. Christ has died so that we need not accept being bad-tempered or a gossip as just part of us; we *can* change.

In contrast to Nabal, Abigail is resourceful, wise, spiritual. Though not perfect; I find her a bit manipulative! She's a smart cookie, though, and she knows how to handle a difficult situation. David might have the high moral ground, but he is on the verge of doing something very wrong. However strong the justification might seem, as soon as we take vengeance into our own hands, we're wrong. Abigail seems to understand David's vulnerable spiritual position here.

Like most of us, David is a mixture of good and evil. In chapter 26 we find him sparing Saul's life on another occasion. But chapter 27 shows him acting in a horrible and ungodly way. He deceives Achish, king of the Philistines, by pretending to be on his side and then doesn't do what he'd said he would in terms of providing defence. And as he travels around he kills people so that no one can report back where he has actually been (27:9). The truth is, David is a man who wants to follow God, but at the same time he's a bloody and brutal warrior who today would be described as a terrorist. If we don't grasp that, we have sanitised the Old Testament. Yet, even in all the horror, God is still meeting with David. God can touch someone whose behaviour is that appalling, that awful.

Of course, we live *this* side of the cross of Jesus, and we have the power and revelation of Jesus to modify our understanding and behaviour. But the Bible doesn't pull its punches over the fact that David is a murderer and an adulterer, an incredible mixture of heaven and hell. He is no plaster saint. Some people would like to believe that the characters in the Old Testament spent their time smelling

This is not because God is a killjoy, but because he wants us to be safe.

Saul goes to a medium who is working under cover and asks her to conjure up Samuel in some occultic celebration. Saul is desperate for advice. Samuel – or a spirit faking Samuel – appears. Saul is totally out of order in doing this, and Samuel gives him some very bad news – far more than he bargained for. He is almost killed by the shock (28:20). This is life at its most desperate. Saul is so anxious, so longing for power, he'll do anything to keep the kingdom – anything but the right thing.

Some people would like to believe that the characters in the Old Testament spent their time smelling the flowers and playing Scalextric with their grandchildren

the flowers and playing Scalextric with their grandchildren. It wasn't like that! But, in the most horrible situations, God is still there. If you're going through hell on earth, then God is still present. Amazingly, even in a world which has turned its back on God and his standards, God has not left us alone! He doesn't easily give up and wash his hands of us. God can cope with the rottenness of the worst criminal in the world. And still he loves them! He can cope with David – and he can cope with you.

But it's Saul who makes the ultimate descent into evil. Chapter 28 shows us Saul with the Witch of Endor. This is a tragic story that reveals Saul as desperate, wicked, and broken. He's at the end of his tether, not knowing how to deal with David, feeling the kingdom slipping from him. Previously he has swept the kingdom clear of wizards, mediums, necromancers and witches, because he knows those practices are wrong. Yet now he himself is dabbling in these evils. The Bible stands opposed to any attempt to contact the dead, any kind of spirit forces or occult practices. It calls them 'detestable' (Deuteronomy 18:9–13).

In my experience, when people are sucked into the demonic they are nearly always being destroyed – emotionally, physically, or in some other way. And for Saul the issue isn't just one of meddling in witchcraft. This is about power. Saul needs the power of the living God filling his life, but he's lost it because he has rebelled against God. David does not need to search out the black arts to help him work out how to be king, because the living God is with him. The only route to true power is the filling of the Holy Spirit, the power of Jesus in our lives, and the blood of the Lamb cleansing us. Thank God for the power of the Cross and of the resurrection!

Transition Living Worksheet

9: Descent into evil
1 Samuel 25–28

1 'The church is suffering from a discipleship deficit.' Is this an over-negative description?

_____

_____

• What evidence do you see to support your view?

_____

_____

2 How can we motivate people to move from a position of just head knowledge about God to a living relationship which deeply affects their behaviour?

_____

_____

• What role does the church have here?

_____

_____

• And the Holy Spirit?

_____

_____

3 Do you struggle with Bible heroes being a mix of good and evil, or find it helpful?

_____

_____

_____

4 Can you imagine what provoked Saul to get involved with the medium (chapter 28)?

_____

_____

• Is it easier or harder for someone to explore the occult in our times?

_____

_____

5 Pray together about the challenge of growing as disciples for yourselves and for your local church community.

_____

_____

_____

Transition Living
10: Good end, bad end
1 Samuel 30,31

By the close of 1 Samuel, David has gone from being a sort of ragamuffin rebel leader to king in waiting. Saul has gone from king to rebel against God, and to a life that ends in the most horrific circumstances.

While David is away from his camp, Ziklag, the Amalekites take the opportunity to come and take away all the women, children, and cattle (30:1,2). This is not an act of terrorism and butchery. They are taken away for use later as a bargaining chip. The Amalekites believe that David won't attack them if they've got his wives and children, and might be sold into slavery. The men are talking of stoning David. As is common today, when things go pear-shaped in life the boss gets blamed! Despite the fact that he has led them fantastically well in battle and done an absolutely stunning job in his leadership, they want to stone him because they've lost their families. To David's credit he seeks God (30:6), God directs him to chase after the raiding party, and he's successful in rescuing all who were taken. And even those who hadn't been part of the rescue have a share. In fact this generosity becomes enshrined in law (30:25).

David, of course, is not immune from tragedy himself, even though he is a man of God. Many of us believe, wrongly, that because we are Christians and we walk with God, we are protected from tragedy and disaster. Those who are older and wiser realise that we can all too easily suffer ill health or bereavement, difficulty in the workplace, the stresses of a difficult marriage or the loneliness of singleness, and any number of other human misfortunes. Loving and following Jesus doesn't confine us in a hermetically sealed unit. Most of us neglect our relationship with God until tragedy strikes, and when it does we cry out to him for help and wonder why he feels a long way away. We need to cultivate intimacy with God to help us in the bad times.

So David, who has built intimacy with God, seeks God in the middle of his difficulty. He gets the promise of a positive outcome (30:8). Not all prayers get this result. Years later when David commits adultery with Bathsheba and a child arrives, he prays for the child to live – but the child dies. God is sovereign and mysterious. Sometimes his answer is 'yes' and sometimes it is 'no'.

Look at the little cameo here of an Egyptian being rescued (30:11). He is a sick slave. In the ancient world, if you had to choose between a sick slave and a well cow, you always chose the well cow and let the sick slave die. Life was incredibly cheap, and a sick slave was left behind because he was a drain on you. Yes, the slave gives him some useful intelligence, but David would have found the raiding party sooner or later anyway. It is a simple act of compassion. It's a reminder that David lives in two worlds: the public arena and the private one. We are defined by what we do privately in the small things as well as what we do pub-

and certainly ignominy at the hands of the Philistines. He is beheaded and his body nailed to a wall as an example to others.

This was a man with incredible promise; a man who was anointed, wanting to serve God; a big man; a significant man; a fantastic man! What has gone wrong here?

Most of us neglect our relationship with God until tragedy strikes, and when it does we cry out to him for help and wonder why he feels a long way away

licly in the big things. We remember David for committing adultery or subduing all those armies or killing Goliath. But this little incident reminds us that David's greatness was tested in small acts of compassion.

In chapter 31 the emphasis moves to Saul. We see him trying to involve his armour-bearer in a suicide pact (31:4). The armour-bearer is terrified and refuses, so eventually Saul commits suicide rather than facing possible torture

One of my sadnesses in being a pastor is to know that in any congregation there are those who are moving from intimacy to irrelevance as far as their relationship with God is concerned. Some people sitting in churches today will die disappointed and far from God. Often it's a gradual drift away from the things that matter until our faith has gone cold. But the great thrill for believers who walk with God all their lives is the opportunity to die well. What decisions are you making today that will help you die well and be remembered as one who walked with God?

What decisions are you making today that will help you die well and be remembered as one who walked with God?

Transition Living Worksheet

10: Good end, bad end
1 Samuel 30, 31

1 'Most of us neglect our relationship with God until tragedy strikes.' This may be typical of human nature, but is it inevitable?

_____

_____

• If we want to change it, what can we do?

_____

_____

2 Spend some time in silence considering the current state of your relationship with God. Could it best be described as:

intimate?
lively?
interesting?
strained?
remote?

• Tell God how you feel about it.

_____

_____

_____

3 What have you learned from the life of Saul over these 10 sessions that helps you understand your own faith journey?

_____

_____

• And what from the life of David?

_____

_____

• What have you learned about leadership?

_____

_____

• And friendship?

_____

_____

4 Spend time as a group praying about how to respond in a godly way to areas of transition in:
• your personal life;
• your local church community;
• the life and culture of your nation.

5 Conclude with prayers of thanksgiving and praise, particularly for:
• the powerful Word of God;
• God's unchanging love for us;
• God's sovereign control of our lives and the nations;
• the sense of worth and security that we find in knowing God.

the Word made fresh! -

other titles from Stephen Gaukroger

Revival Living

insights from 1 Timothy for the 3rd millennium church

Paul's been there, done that – and got the t-shirt! He's planted churches all over the ancient world – congregations of living, vibrant believers. He's seen miracles and disappointments. He's experienced success and endured the most incredible opposition. Nearing the end of his days, far from being a spent force, he's still passionately full of joy and faith – and still looking for revival.

Is that our longing? Do we want the cobwebs of our mediocrity to be blown away by the breath of God? Take Paul's advice to Timothy on how to live a godly life, how to set an example as a leader, how to communicate a gospel free from error, how to be the best you can for God.

ISBN 1 84427 042 4

A Code for Living

the Ten Commandments for the 3rd millennium church

Largely forgotten – yet hugely foundational. Dismissed by many as ancient rules irrelevant today, the Ten Commandments are of vital and practical importance to the way society operates, providing an essential framework for how we relate to God and to each other in fulfilling ways.

But aren't they a 'mission impossible'? True, none of us can keep all the commandments all the time. The only way to obey these laws is through a new power and a new heart that's part of knowing Jesus. We need to rediscover why the Ten Commandments are so potentially enriching to us as individuals and communities.

ISBN 1 84427 041 6

Available from Christian bookshops or from Scripture Union Mail Order:
PO Box 5148, Milton Keynes MLO, MK2 2YX, tel 01908 856006 or online through www.scriptureunion.org.uk

church@home

SU's online magazine for the world of small groups

• ready-to-use sessions to try • inspirational articles • 'how to' features

• case studies on real groups • reports of best practice • your space for your say

• info on training and resources

www.scriptureunion.org.uk/churchathome

the one-stop shop for all your small group needs

CONNECT BIBLE STUDIES

Innovative small groups studies that help interpret contemporary culture in the light of Biblical insights. Engage with popular books, TV programmes, music and film. Four themes, four sessions in each.

Over 20 titles available, including:

Harry Potter	Lord of the Rings
The Matrix	The Simpsons
Billy Elliot	James Bond 007
TV Game Shows	Friends
Madonna	John Grisham's Thrillers

A JOURNEY OF THE HEART

THE PILGRIM'S GUIDE TO PRAYER

Kate Hayes

Do you find prayer a welcome time of personal space? A tedious duty? An adventure? An embarrassment? A struggle with concentration? Uplifting? Confusing? Intimidating?

Do you see it as a skill to be practised? An art to perfect? An exercise to be endured? As natural as breathing? As tricky as skateboarding?

If you want to explore what it means to pray with purpose, growing in understanding of and intimacy with your God, this series of six Bible-based studies – which can be tackled in a small group or on your own – will take you on a rewarding journey.

Ideal for Lent – but great at other times, too! Includes sections on:

* praying alone
* praying with and for others
* praying about difficult decisions
* praying in the tough times
* fasting

ISBN 1 85999 797 X

These and many other small group resources from Scripture Union are available from Christian bookshops or from Scripture Union Mail Order: PO Box 5148, Milton Keynes MLO, MK2 2YX, tel 01908 856006 or online through www.scriptureunion.org.uk

SCRIPTURE UNION
USING THE BIBLE TO INSPIRE CHILDREN, YOUNG PEOPLE AND ADULTS TO KNOW GOD